SuBo's CAT

The Imaginings Of Susan Boyle's Pampered Pussy

Illustrations by Anastasia Catris

HarperCollinsPublishers
77–85 Fulham Palace Road,
Hammersmith, London W6 8JB
www.harpercollins.co.uk

First published by HarperCollins Publishers 2010

This book is not endorsed by, or associated in any way with,
Susan Boyle or any other individuals who may appear in it.
Including Pebbles.

10 9 8 7 6 5 4 3 2 1

A catalogue record of this book is available from the British Library

ISBN 978-0-00-737612-4

Printed and bound in China.

Pebbles would like to thank Anna Valentine, Hannah Black, Anastasia Catris and all of the staff at HarperCollins for helping her to write her moggy memoirs. She would also like to thank the Catris family for supplying an ideal ghost writer. Most importantly she would like to thank her owner, Susan Boyle, for being such a good sport...(hopefully!)

...AAMAAAAAAZIIIIIIIIIIIIIIIINNNNGGGGGG GRRRRRRRAAAACCCCEEEE...
CATS
PHANTOM
LES MISERABLES

AUDITION CDs

53

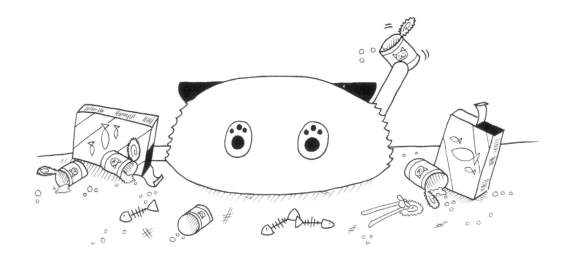

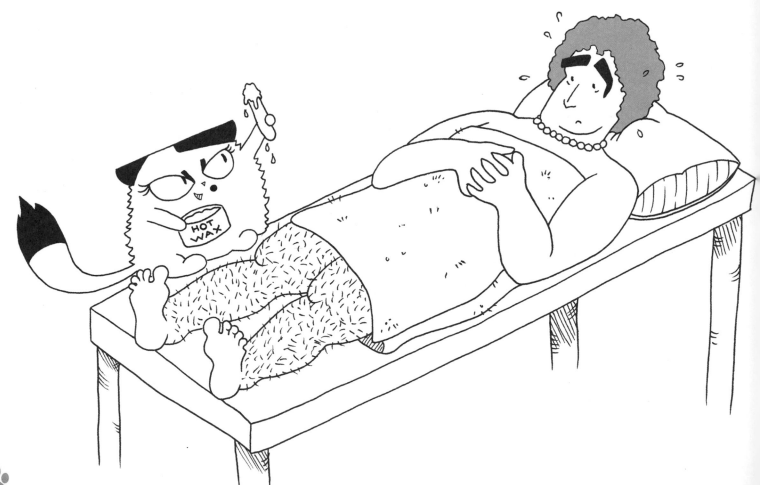

PAMPAWS
CREAM

SUSAN BOYLE : I DREAMED A DREAM

EWS JUST IN: SuBo AND PEBBLES SPLIT!!! — UP NEXT: THE WEATHER

Loose
Pussy... PEBBLES: "SUBO FORGETS THAT I MADE HER WHO SHE IS!!!"

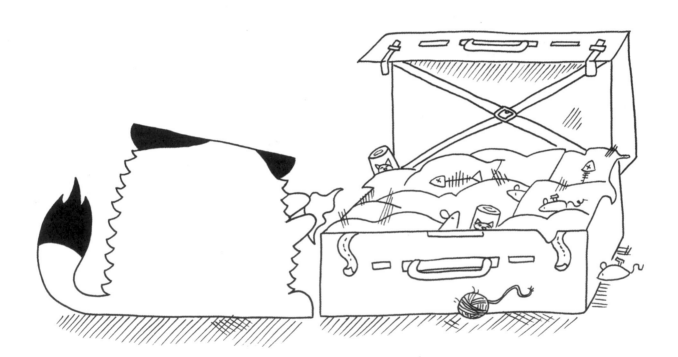

111